BOOKWORMS

The Making of Everyday Things

Baseballs

Derek Miller

Cavendish Square
New York

Published in 2020 by Cavendish Square Publishing, LLC
243 5th Avenue, Suite 136, New York, NY 10016

First Edition

Website: cavendishsq.com

Library of Congress Cataloging-in-Publication Data

Names: Miller, Derek, author.
Title: Baseballs / Derek Miller.
Description: New York : Cavendish Square, 2020. | Series: The making of everyday things | Includes index. | Audience: K to Grade 3.
Identifiers: LCCN 2018043481 (print) | LCCN 2018044662 (ebook) | ISBN 9781502646859 (ebook) | ISBN 9781502646842 (library bound) | ISBN 9781502646828 (pbk.) | ISBN 9781502646835 (6 pack)
Subjects: LCSH: Baseballs--Juvenile literature.
Classification: LCC GV875.2 (ebook) | LCC GV875.2 .M55 2020 (print) | DDC 796.357--dc23
LC record available at https://lccn.loc.gov/2018043481

Editorial Director: David McNamara
Copy Editor: Nathan Heidelberger
Associate Art Director: Alan Sliwinski
Designer: Ginny Kemmerer
Production Coordinator: Karol Szymczuk
Photo Research: J8 Media

The photographs in this book are used by permission and through the courtesy of: Cover Guzel Studio/Shutterstock.com; p. 5 Hello RF Zcool/Shutterstock.com; p. 7 Matt Brown/iStockphoto.com; p. 9 DeAgostini/Getty Images; p. 11 Michael Doolittle/Alamy Stock Photo; p. 13 FabrikaSimf/Shutterstock.com; p. 15 Mary Knox Merrill/The Christian Science Monitor/Getty Images; p. 17 Tim Clayton/Corbis/Getty Images; p. 19 Julie Alissi/J8 Media; p. 21 B51/Mark Brown/Getty Images.

Printed in the United States of America

Contents

Baseballs look simple.

They are not.

They have many layers.

All the layers are important.

Baseballs need to bounce.

Players hit them.

The baseballs bounce off the bat.

How they are made helps baseballs bounce.

The center of the baseball
is **cork**.

Cork comes from special trees.

Cork is their bark.

Cork is strong.

The cork keeps its shape.

Baseballs stay round.

There is **rubber** around the cork.

You can see rubber in rubber bands.

Rubber is very bouncy.

Rubber helps the baseball bounce off the bat.

Yarn covers the rubber.

Yarn is like string.

It is light and soft.

It makes the baseball bigger and softer.

The cover of the baseball
is leather.

Stitches hold the leather
together.

Stitches are the red threads.

Stitches do not look special.

But they are very important.

They help the ball spin
through the air.

They let pitchers throw
curve balls.

H

All the layers work together.

Baseballs need all of them.

The layers let baseballs bounce off the bat.

The layers let baseballs spin through the air!

Rawlings
OFFICIAL
MAJOR LEAGUE BASEBALL

New Words

cork (CORK) A strong material made from a special tree.

rubber (RUHB-er) A stretchy or bouncy material.

stitches (STICH-is) The red strings on a baseball.

yarn (YAHRN) A long string used to make something.

Index

About the Author

Derek Miller is a teacher and writer. He likes to learn interesting facts about things we see every day.

About BOOKWORMS

Bookworms help independent readers gain reading confidence through high-frequency words, simple sentences, and strong picture/text support. Each book explores a concept that helps children relate what they read to the world they live in.